INSPIRING LIVES

SCOTT JOPLIN
King of Ra

By Mary Ann Hoffman

Gareth Stevens
Publishing

Please visit our Web site www.garethstevens.com. For a free color catalog of all our high-quality books, call toll free 1-800-542-2595 or fax 1-877-542-2596.

Library of Congress Cataloging-in-Publication Data

Hoffman, Mary Ann, 1947-
Scott Joplin : king of ragtime / Mary Ann Hoffman.
    p. cm. — (Inspiring lives)
Includes index.
ISBN 978-1-4339-3632-6 (pbk.)
ISBN 978-1-4339-3633-3 (6-pack)
ISBN 978-1-4339-3631-9 (library binding)
1. Joplin, Scott, 1868-1917—Juvenile literature. 2. Composers—United States—
Biography—Juvenile literature. I. Title.
ML3930.J66H64 2010
780.92—dc22
[B]

                        2009037376

Published in 2010 by Gareth Stevens Publishing
111 East 14th Street, Suite 349
New York, NY 10003

Designer: Daniel Hosek
Editor: Mary Ann Hoffman

Photo credits: Cover (Joplin), p. 1 (Joplin) © Redferns/Getty Images; cover (background), pp. 1 (music covers), 19, 27, 29 Wikimedia Commons; pp. 5, 15 © Hulton Archive/Getty Images; pp. 7 (all images), 11, 25 Shutterstock.com; pp. 9, 17 iStock.com; p. 13 © Buccina Studios/Photodisc/Getty Images; p. 21 © Michael Ochs Archive/Getty Images; p. 23 © Walter Sanders/Time & Life Pictures/Getty Images.

Printed in the United States of America

CPSIA compliance information: Batch #CW10GS: For further information contact Gareth Stevens, New York, New York at 1-800-542-2595.

Contents

Meet Scott Joplin

Scott Joplin was born in northeast Texas around 1868. His family moved to Texarkana when he was young.

TEXAS

Texarkana

Austin

Scott Learns About Music

Scott's father played the violin. His mother played the banjo.

violin

banjo

Scott liked music. He wanted to learn how to play, too.

Playing the Banjo

Scott learned to play the banjo. He liked making music with the strings.

Playing the Piano

Scott took piano lessons when he was young.

Scott liked to play the piano. He played for his family and friends.

Writing Music

Scott wrote and played music. He played his music on a piano.

Scott had to work very hard. He played in many different places. He played during the world's fair in Chicago in 1893.

Ragtime

Scott moved to Sedalia, Missouri, in 1895. He wrote and played a kind of music called ragtime.

When Scott played ragtime, people liked to dance.

Some of Scott's music was put on piano rolls. The rolls were put into a special piano. The piano played the music by itself !

piano roll

Well-Known Songs

Scott wrote many songs. Two famous songs are the "Maple Leaf Rag" and "The Entertainer."

King of Ragtime!

Scott Joplin is known as the "King of Ragtime"! He died in 1917.

Timeline

around 1868 Scott is born.

1893 Scott plays in Chicago.

1895 Scott moves to Sedalia, Missouri.

1899 Scott writes the "Maple Leaf Rag."

1902 Scott writes "The Entertainer."

1917 Scott dies.

For More Information

Books:

Bankton, John. *The Life and Times of Scott Joplin.* Hockessin, DE: Mitchell Lane Publishers, Inc., 2005.

Hubbard-Brown, Janet. *Scott Joplin: Composer.* New York: Chelsea House, 2006.

Sabir, C. Ogbu. *Scott Joplin: The King of Ragtime.* Chanhassen, MN: Child's World, 2001.

Web Sites:

A Biography of Scott Joplin

www.scottjoplin.org/biography.htm

Scott Joplin

www.incwell.com/Biographies/Joplin.html

Glossary

banjo: a musical instrument with a long neck, round body, and strings

entertainer: a person who plays, sings, acts, or dances for the enjoyment of others

piano roll: a roll of paper with holes that makes piano keys move by themselves

ragtime: a lively kind of music usually played on a piano

violin: a musical instrument with four strings that is usually held against the chin and played with a bow

world's fair: a fair in which many countries take part

Index